THE DIVISIVE DECADE

BY
PETER L. EDMEAD

EDITED BY
KATHRYNE WRAY AND MARTIN FLYNN

The Divisive Decade
©1999 Peter Edmead

CIP catalogue record for this book is available from the British Library.

ISBN 0 7093 02290

Published by Birmingham Library Services.

Designed and produced by Birmingham City Council, CSO Design & Print 0121 303 1986.

Photograph credits

Front cover: A Red Cross worker helps a young West Indian immigrant who has something in her eye 1956, Hulton Getty
        Images
Back cover: Birmingham Central Library Dyche Collection

Other photographs courtesy of Birmingham Central Library Dyche Collection, Hulton Getty Images, Ben Bennie, Enos Clarke, Eloise Crichlow, Frederick Dorsett, Agnes Dupont, Edgar and Ena Edmead, Charles Edmeade, Meryck Edwards, Wilfred Greaves, George Henry, Lacess and Lloyd King, Samuel 'Sonny' Philips, Delatris and Hazel Thomas, Bernice and John Walters, Aldith Warner, Ferdinand 'Motion' Williams.

CONTENTS

ACKNOWLEDGEMENTS

I must take this opportunity to convey my thanks to all of the people who have helped me complete this book. Obvious thanks go to my parents, Edgar and Ena Edmead, my sister Elyniss and brothers George, Gene, Colin and Lorne. Also to all of my friends, particularly those from the Small Heath area of Birmingham, they are too numerous to mention but they know who they are. My thanks go out to all of the people that I met during my time at Sheffield - particularly Steve Williams and Barclay O'Malley my two sparring partners at the Croft House boxing gymnasium in the centre of Sheffield. My thanks also go to the old fairground fighter Bob Birney, who was the proprietor of the gymnasium. To the other people that I met in Sheffield big thanks to Will Hunter, for being a friend. This book is also a tribute to all of my teachers. To my original teachers Mr. Tom Clitheroe and Dr. John Mason go my thanks for setting me off on this long road. To all of my tutors at university a mention is richly deserved. At the University of Sheffield I would like to thank Professors Colin Holmes, Ian Kershaw, William Leatherbarrow and Dr. Robert Cook for their support and encouragement. No lesser thanks go to Dr. Mathew Thomson, at the University of Warwick and to the staff at the University of Birmingham. These include Professor Christopher Wickham, Dr. W. Scott Lucas, Dr. E. Arfon Rees, Dr. Nicholas Cull and, of course, Dr. Carl Chinn. I would also like to thank the Leisure Services Department of Birmingham City Council for producing this book, particularly the editor Martin Flynn for the faith that he showed in me. My thanks also go to two people in the Revenues Department of Birmingham City Council, Barry Powell and Fitzroy Pencil for allowing me to access their facilities. I should also like to thank Matthew Walters and John Sorohan, without whose help the writing of this book would have proved a much more difficult task. Finally my gratitude goes to all of the original oral sources for giving me their time and their precious pictorial memories for reproduction. Last but not least I must thank the two ladies in my life for supporting me through all of this. To Mina "The Girl From Mars" and Zoya "The New Kid in Town" go all my love.

Peter L. Edmead 1999

INTRODUCTION

The Dyche Collection, Birmingham Central Library

Ever since the post-war movement of Caribbean immigrants to Great Britain there has been a continuous debate regarding the significance of their arrival. This debate has proved to be fraught with difficulty and ultimately has led to some serious questioning of the supposed tradition of British tolerance.

The victory of the Allied forces in 1945 and the ensuing peace resulted in a post-war period of consolidation throughout Western Europe. With a significant level of assistance from the United States government Britain was able to rebuild its national economy and bask in the afterglow of its 1945 victory. Full employment became a central issue for all political parties and was necessary if Britain wished to prevent any future social and economic ills. This was anticipated by Beveridge's *Report on Social Insurance and Allied Services* (1942) and the Education Act of 1944. At the workplace, however, as the indigenous population climbed up the economic and social ladder there emerged a large void for low-skilled manual employment. Consequently, in order to sustain a climate of economic buoyancy, the leaders of the day turned to their West Indian Commonwealth subjects to fill these vacancies.

With the supposed 'pull' factor of economic betterment, and 'push' factors, such as economic stagnation and the underdeveloped conditions on the islands which prevailed at the time, it was thought that there would be no shortage of West Indians to take advantage of the opportunities on offer.

Subsequently, on June 22nd 1948, the former German troopship 'Empire Windrush' sailed into Tilbury Docks, Essex, carrying some four hundred and ninety two migrants from Jamaica to Great Britain. Thus it would seem that Caribbean immigration into Great Britain had begun.

The traditionally accepted version of events infers that although the immigrants were faced with some difficulties, such as the upheaval of moving thousands of miles to a new land, they were generally welcomed by their hosts. It was felt that there was some limited discrimination, which often posed difficulties for those trying to find rooms and employment, but this was seen as the exception rather than the rule. It was not until 1952 when the Americans passed their McCarren-Walter Immigration Act, which severely limited the entry of West Indians into the United States, that immigration became an issue of government concern in Great Britain.

Matters came to a sad conclusion in 1958 when white racists, who could not bring themselves to accept the newcomers, took to the streets of Notting Hill and Nottingham. The outcome was Britain's first urban riots since the anti-Jewish Battle of Cable Street in the East End of London in 1936.

This account presents a simplistic view, which was in fact accepted by many in Great Britain, particularly during the late 1940s. Indeed it was not until the middle 1980s, with books such as Colin Holmes' *John Bull's Island*, that this crude orthodox account began to be challenged.

It could be argued that this simplistic view was mainly due to a confused and often misguided understanding of the concept of immigration. Until this point the common perception of immigration had always related to a massive influx of people with no racial or national distinction. Also, as there was no set government policy at this time, immigration was seen as an improvised happening with no apparent pattern. Unfortunately the end result of this was that the impact of immigration was either overstated or ignored depending on the viewpoint adopted.

The inescapable fact was that the British

public had a distorted view of the pattern of immigration into Britain. As Tony Kushner points out, an examination of the number of arrivals during the ten years after Empire Windrush reveals that the Irish were by far the largest group of immigrants. Yet, since they did not share the dark complexions of their West Indian counterparts they did not have the attention of the British public forced upon them.[1]

Extroopship 'Empire Windrush' with 492 migrants from Jamaica aboard, June 1948, Hulton Getty Images.

Contemporary studies of immigrant communities in Cardiff and Stepney, which were undertaken by a school of anthropologists who worked from

Edinburgh University seemed only to cloud the issue even further. Although studies of these port areas illustrated a wealth of information on immigrants, they only examined the wider immigration phenomenon and did not give any attention to the specific area of Caribbean immigration. As Duffield asserts:

The true pioneers of the history of blacks in Britain were social scientists mainly interested in the matters of contemporary race relations, but with a weather eye for black and white relations in the British past.[2]

Consequently, they provided the false theory that immigration inevitably led to a divided 'magpie' or black/white society. The end result is that we are left with a simple one-dimensional interpretation of Caribbean immigration which is patently flawed; a notion which is reiterated by Holmes:

We can easily lay our hands on texts which portray Britain as a society in which hostility towards immigrants and refugees has been rampant and universal and remains so. In fact, however, attitudes and actions at both official and popular level have often displayed a complexity which cautions against any simple categorisation of responses.[3]

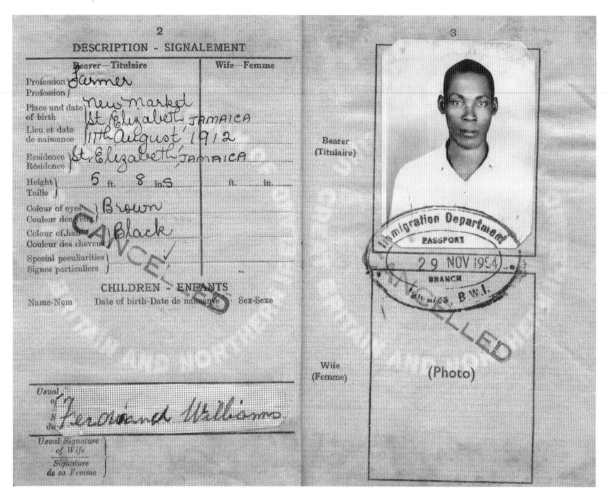

Ferdinand 'Motion' Williams' Jamaican Passport, 1954

A major thread of this complex web which was overlooked is that, from the onset, Caribbean immigration was not a uniform or controlled occurrence. The arrival of four hundred and ninety two people on Empire Windrush in 1948 may well have been numerically the largest single arrival of immigrants from the Caribbean, however, it was only a symbolic event in the history of Caribbean immigration and was by no means the beginning.

The 'Divisive Decade' seeks to destroy the myth that the Windrush episode of 1948 was the start of Caribbean immigration. It aims to challenge the often simple interpretation of events presented by many traditional accounts of the ten years in question, and wherever possible seeks to convey the motives and actions of both Caribbean immigrants and hosts alike.

References

(1) Kushner, T. Writing in Johnson, P. 20th Century Britain. (1994)
(2) Duffield, I. Article. 'History and Historians' in 'Blacks in Britain'. History Today September (1981) p.34
(3) Holmes, C. Writing in Pooley and White. Migrants, Emigrants and Immigrants. (1991) pp.202-203

BACKGROUND TO ARRIVAL

In the West Indies during the 1930s various workers revolts took place, particularly in Jamaica, which threatened Britain's colonial economic grip over the region. The main focus of the workers' anger was the various subsidiary companies of the British sugar manufacturer Tate & Lyle. Even on smaller islands such as St. Kitts there was serious concern that wage levels had remained stagnant, workers were being laid off at will, and reinvestment in the region did not appear to be forthcoming: 'every British governor called for warships, marines and aeroplanes, total casualties in the British colonies amounted to 29 dead, 115 wounded.'[1]

Yet in spite of this, the common bond which continued to hold the Caribbean people together was their idea of the 'British Nation' being their 'Mother Country'. This idea of 'Nation' goes deeper than just the colonial experience. Having arrived as bondsmen to their white captors centuries before from Africa, and then living on the islands as part of a mixed yet relatively harmonious community comprising of Blacks, Whites and Asians, the idea of nation which many West Indians clung to was one of a British heritage. This was in part due to the glorification of the British Empire, as

The Dyche Collection, Birmingham Central Library

The Dyche Collection, Birmingham Central Library

Edgar Edmead remembers:

We were always taught at school in the 1920s and 1930s that the sun never set twice in the empire, since the empire was so vast anywhere it set would be a part of that said empire.

The outbreak of World War Two in 1939 reinforced these sentiments. An act of hypocrisy on behalf of the 'Mother Nation' is the only way to describe the events which followed, as Douglas and

Bousquet point out:

Those who had been shot at by British troops for proclaiming their rights as citizens of the Empire would now be expected to shoot with British troops at a European enemy. This they loyally did.[2]

As West Indian personnel enlisted to fight, as England expected, there was confusion in their minds as to the role they were to play in the war. Their belief was that they were fighting to aid the 'Mother Country' against the Nazi threat and yet the Ministry of Labour had advertised widely throughout the West Indies to fill civilian posts back in Britain. These calls for labour were enthusiastically and loyally met by West Indian workers entering Britain. As Gilkes declares: 'many joined the Red Cross and other services in spite of the persistence of a colour bar and overt racial prejudice.'[3]

Unacceptable social conditions and instances of overt racial prejudice were glibly explained away as an extension of the American concept 'Jim Crow' (a form of apartheid). The central focus of this concept was a 'separate but equal' relationship between the races in America, an idea which gained credence after the celebrated Plessy v Ferguson case of 1896.

West Indian personnel, however, were not prepared to accept this attitude which prevailed in wartime Britain and indeed it only served to further challenge their belief in Great Britain as a bastion of moral guidance and leadership. The Jamaican serviceman Lloyd King recalls:

I came over from Jamaica to join the RAF in 1944. We were originally based at that large Butlins camp at Filey in North Yorkshire. My new West Indian friends and I could not begin to believe the very bad way that the Black American soldiers were being treated both by their own people and by the English. We were from the Caribbean and we soon teamed up together, us, Bajans (people from Barbados), Trinidadians and so on. We Caribbeans are resourceful people. The Americans may have been running their own kind of apartheid at the time but we all made sure that we would stand no nonsense from them, or the English.

A very public incident which illustrated that racial discrimination was taking place on all levels occurred in 1943. This involved the West Indian cricket captain Learie Constantine, who at the time was working as welfare officer for Ernest Bevin's Ministry of Labour. Constantine had been asked to captain a West Indies guest side at Lords, yet when he and his family attempted to book into the

Imperial Hotel in Russell Square, London, they were asked to leave because it was thought that their presence might upset the white American soldiers who were residing there. The following year Constantine won a civil law suit against the hotel.

Lloyd King in RAF uniform 1944

Events such as this served only to reinforce the already widespread anger amongst West Indians in wartime Great Britain. As Bousquet reports, 'there was war on the streets of several of those northern cities because, especially the Jamaicans, they didn't think twice about putting the Americans in their place.'[4] The often hostile actions of the British and American servicemen only succeeded in promoting an even stronger bond of solidarity amongst the West Indian troops. As Lloyd King remembers:

We heard that some of our lads took a beating one night at a bar in Preston. The following evening there was an attempt to put a curfew on our movement but we organised ourselves. We were like they were, in uniform, so the authorities could hardly stop us going out. This was because we knew that the white servicemen would be back there. There was chaos that night as they could not understand the fact that we had come back with even numbers. The pub workers were sheltering behind the oak bar as we took our revenge and wrecked their pub. After that they did not mess about with us again.

Prime Minister Winston Churchill also displayed entrenched prejudices over the race issue. His understanding of this issue was based upon theories from the Eugenic debate, which still prevailed at the turn of the century.[5] His ignorance of the Negro position was clearly illustrated when he was told about an incident involving a black official from the colonial office who had always lunched at a certain restaurant, and now was barred because the restaurant was being patronised by white American officers. The Prime Minister's reply was:

"That's all right, if he takes a banjo with him they'll think he's one of the band".[6]

Lloyd and Lacess King's wedding at St. Germain's Church, Edgbaston 1955

Traditional British accounts of the Second World War often stress how the Allies worked together. Yet West Indian personnel had a rather different experience, and also a particular perception of how their alleged colonial superiors viewed them as people. Great Britain's need for labour during and after the war was seen by many West Indians as a way of avoiding the poor economic condition that these same British had left their region in since the days of the West

Indian slave system. A contradictory situation had arisen whereby Britain would be forced to turn to its colonies for wage labour. Great Britain, however, still maintained that the 'newcomers' were merely facilitating post-war redevelopment. Britain believed that ultimately this would benefit the lands that these people had left; the truth was a different matter.

The Dyche Collection, Birmingham Central Library

In the aftermath of World War Two there emerged a great need to rebuild the nation particularly as Britain still imagined itself as a leading world power. Historical accounts still maintain that

there was a continuity of government policy to encourage immigrant workers. As Grenville points out:

'West Indians, the Blacks from the colonies and the islands had all been welcomed as fighting men during the war, and after 1945 West Indian labour was encouraged to come to Britain to fill jobs for which there were not sufficient whites'.[7]

Contrary to popular belief, however, there is no evidence to suggest that after the war, particularly between 1945 and 1948, West Indians were encouraged to enter Great Britain to find employment. As Lloyd King remembers: "The war was done and I returned to Jamaica in 1946".

The nature of post-war immigration from the West Indies was complex. Some Caribbean war personnel saw the possibility to remain in Great Britain as an attractive option, yet many traditional accounts are often misguided in their commentaries on this sequence of events, as Hennessy states:

The authorities could not compel the Caribbean servicemen to leave at the end of the war, but they were encouraged to return home and free passages were laid on as an incentive.[8]

After the war there was a recruitment

drive throughout Europe for volunteer workers to enter Britain under the European Voluntary Workers Scheme (E.V.W.S). The volunteers consisted primarily of former war prisoners, political refugees and Polish war personnel. Anwar reports that:

They were engaged for three years for a specific job chosen by the Ministry of Labour and could be expelled at any time for misconduct. Accidents or ill health were also likely to lead to deportation. They were compelled to belong to a Trade Union, they could not be promoted over British workers, and they would be the first to be made redundant if such situations arose.[9]

Even the 1949 Royal Commission on Population called for any future migrations of workers into Great Britain to be of 'white stock'. Apparently this was to allow their easy assimilation into the community:

The Royal Commission on Population in 1949 had declared, with what seemed later to be complacent superiority, that immigration could only be welcomed without reserve if the migrants were of good human stock, and were not prevented by their religion or race from intermarrying with the host population and becoming emerged in it.[10]

The biggest irony of all is exemplified in the fact that during the time when post-war immigration policy was being adopted, potential Caribbean migrants who held a British passport had more legal right than any other group to enter and settle in this country. The passing of the British Nationality Act in 1948 meant that West Indians were now legally able to reside in Great Britain. From the evidence presented so far the traditional image of Great Britain welcoming Caribbean labour in the late 1940s was not a correct interpretation of the situation.

References

(1) Williams, E. From Columbus to Castro: The History of the Caribbean 1492-1969. (1993) pp. 473-474
(2) Bousquet, B. and Douglas, C. West Indian Women at Work (1991) p.43
(3) Gilkes, M. The Making of Britain (1988) p.149
(4) Bousquet, B. and Douglas, C. Ibid. pp.77-78 Also see Toole, J. 'GIs and the Race Bar in Wartime Warrington' in History Today July (1993)
(5) Wooldridge, A. 'In a Place of Fear' in The Making of Britain: Echoes of Greatness (1988)
(6) Roberts, A. Eminent Churchillians (1994) p.214
(7) Grenville, J. The Collins History of the World in the Twentieth Century. (1994) p.504
(8) Hennessy, P. Never Again Britain 1945-1951 (1993) p.439
(9) Anwar, M. Race and Politics. (1986) p.7
(10) Madgewick, Steeds Williams. Britain Since 1945 (1982) p.321

TRAVELLING JUST TO FIND WORK

West Indian immigrants came to Great Britain for a variety of reasons. It must, however, be stressed that immigration was not a new phenomenon in their culture. Following the era of slavery, there was a strong urge amongst the West Indian population to migrate in search of work. Central America's great civil engineering feat, the Panama Canal, would not have been completed without migrant Jamaican labour. Kenneth Spencer bears this point out:

My parents moved to Cuba with me when I was three months old. He was a stevedore and she was a washerwoman. I came back to Jamaica at aged nineteen and went straight away to America, in 1940, to work on a farm in Buffalo. I returned there again as part of the war effort so coming to Great Britain was only what I was accustomed to. The only thing I have not found is that street that was supposed to be paved with gold.

The migratory trait of the people of the region was exemplified again 'during the 1930s, (when) for example, there was heavy immigration from overcrowded, economically depressed Barbados to land rich, under-populated British Guiana(Guyana).'[1]

Edgar Edmead 1956

It would seem that most immigrants harboured a natural human yearning for financial betterment and adventure and that this was what made them emigrate to British shores. Yet this feeling, according to Edgar Edmead is not strictly true:

The English think we only came over here because we thought that this was a superior way of life. That is rubbish. Back home in

St. Kitts there were always people going to work on the oil refineries of Aruba and Curaçao for long periods of time. At that time though you needed a permit so that is why I came over here. I viewed it initially as a way of seeing another place and to aid my family back home financially. I did not really want to leave there but I saw it as a short-term thing.

This sentiment, although popular amongst many migrants, only tells a part of the story. For others there was a feeling that the economies of the West Indies were stagnating and this was their chance to better themselves. As George Henry comments:

I had a trade back home as a driver. So nobody could say that I came over here to learn anything. The point was that the white man was always taking from us back there and did not seem to want to reinvest the profits in the region. So I decided to come over here where I did not expect it to be easy, but I thought I might be in a better position to secure a future financially.

Some critics point to the fact that many immigrants said that they were initially intending to stay for only a few years and query why these people did not return to the West Indies if their experiences were so unpalatable. Their arguments, however, have some serious flaws. Upon arrival employment was sought and then gained. Once there was a regular income this enabled wives and offspring to come over to Britain. The money from employment helped to secure a mortgage and the well-being of the family unit continued to develop naturally. In time the original five-year plan evaporated as the unit built a future in the new surroundings for the parents and older children. Continuity was maintained as the new country was considered home for the younger members of the family unit and there ensued a familial division of loyalty when considering what constituted 'home'. Wilfred Greaves sums this up:

The English do not understand how we feel. How can we just go back and leave what we have built in England. Our children were born here, live here, and will remain here. Barbados is in my head, in my memory.

It can be argued that as early as the mid-1940s Britain's relationship with its colonies was under pressure. The reason for this was that by the 1920s New York had replaced London as the centre of world capital finance. So although Britain still considered itself a major leader in the world, and also in the West Indies, it could not help noticing the financial investment that American companies were putting into the neighbouring larger Spanish-speaking Caribbean islands of Puerto Rico, Cuba and the Dominican Republic. Britain began losing its prior dominant position particularly due to rival American investment. Britain's economic situation was made worse by the Second World War which left the United States in a far superior financial position. The reality of the 1940s was that Britain was floundering in its attempts to maintain a world role. As Hennessy points out:

It should not be thought that this (immigration) was the result of any rational cost-benefit analysis of Empire...It arose from squalor and neglect in the British West Indies and collapse of sugar prices in the inter-war period which led to a series of riots. [2]

References
(1) Gilkes, M. Ibid. p.146
(2) Hennessy, P. Ibid. p.221

Birmingham Corporation Transport uniform. The Dyche Collection, Birmingham Central Library

THE JOURNEY OVER
AND FIRST IMPRESSIONS

Immigration was a varied experience for many Caribbean immigrants and it is helpful to analyse the motives of these people who were leaving their native land. To some, such as Ena Edmead, the journey over to Great Britain was a great happening:

Ena Edmead 1956

For most of us on my journey the boat was like a party. I, for one, was glad to be leaving there. A bricklayer from St. Kitts called Arnold Smithen was in such a jolly mood that when he ran out of liquor to drink he stole and drank my only bottle of Bay Rum. I was so mad, for I was sure that I could not purchase Bay Rum in England.

Not all immigrants, however, were so sure, as Edgar Edmead recalls:

I always thought that this would be a short-term thing. As I recall, on my ship I am sure that I signed a document which I thought would allow me to stay in Britain for just five years. That, I thought, would allow me the time to build up some capital in order to return home.

Some immigrants who travelled later argued that peer pressure also influenced their decision to leave the islands. This is illustrated by Eloise Crichlow's experience:

I was working in the Roman Catholic college in Barbados during the 1950s and pay and conditions were good. I did not have to come over to Great Britain for any economic reasons. However, a lot of my friends had made the trip so I was anxious that I may be left over there. I flew from Sewell Airport to London, then made my way to Birmingham. Even though I was lucky in that I hadn't got to find digs with any strangers my first reaction was 'give me Barbados' all the time.

Not all immigrants were enthusiastic about settling in Great Britain, as is illustrated. Some felt that parental pressure also played a role in their decision to leave. Enos Clarke remembers:

My parents were always telling me that they were going to send me over to finish my education in Great Britain. They said that the education system was bound to be better than the one in Jamaica. I did not want to go to Great Britain. Britain, I thought, was a place always at war. I did not want to be walking down the road and have a bomb land near me! That is how naive I was about Britain.

Others left, not willingly, but in order to respect their parents' wishes. Lloyd King recalls:

It was late 1950 to 1951 and I had been keeping in touch with some of my colleagues from the war. They were writing to me and telling me of their intentions to migrate to Great Britain or to the United

Eloise Crichlow, Thursfield Studios, Small Heath 1960

States. My memories of the British and the Americans were not nice ones. I remember their conduct towards us during the war so neither country recommended itself to me. However, at the time I was having a lot of trouble with my relationships with women. My parents thought it best if I were to also emigrate and one evening when I came home the ticket for the boat was there waiting for me. It was 1951 and here I was back in England.

Other West Indian immigrants felt that

emigrating to Britain would provide them with the opportunity to form a new identity. For many it was more than just a three thousand mile journey; it was in fact a complete break from the past. Some registered their passports in their mother's name. Others, such as separated women who were travelling with their offspring, made sure that their passports carried their maiden name, and many immigrants even changed their name completely in preparation for what they hoped would be a new life in the 'Mother Country'. For many West Indians the 'Mother Country' was hailed as the 'New Jerusalem', a land where justice and equal opportunity prevailed.[1]

In Great Britain during the 1950s economic hardship was becoming an issue of growing concern, and was lasting much longer than many had expected or hoped for. The majority of the British population saw this influx of immigrants as something which would only put further pressure on the already financially strained economy. Unfortunately the sad result of this was that the immigrants who arrived in Great Britain were judged suspiciously and often treated badly by the indigenous population, who displayed what can only be described as characteristic hypocrisy.

Hunt reiterates this thought:

Is it not the height of racial arrogance to argue that a coloured man who comes to Britain to build a better life for himself and his family is a wastrel and a scrounger while an Englishman who emigrates to Australia or New Zealand for the same purpose is hailed as a pioneer with the noblest intentions.[2]

An identifiable factor which sets apart the immigration pattern of the 1950s from the continual, though not as numerically large, Negro migrations of the past is that these immigrants did not settle exclusively in Britain's port areas, such as Bristol, Cardiff and Liverpool, as had previously been the case. Banton records that:

The inland movement to the industrial cities, where, since the war, employment opportunities have been at their best and the housing situation especially unfavourable, indicates a new phase in the history of Negro immigrants in Britain.[3]

The immigrants were expected to assimilate into regular working hours, novel travelling arrangements and somewhat different eating habits, all of which were part of an environment that was far removed from the rural lifestyle which many had been accustomed to on the islands. On arriving in this 'strange' host country a mixture of first

Agnes and Spencer Dupont's wedding at Villa Road Methodist Church, Handsworth 1958. Spencer Dupont and his sister Ruby Woodley (to the right of his wife) are both native West Indians.

impressions emerged. A sentiment expressed by one immigrant portrays how immediate and almost comical many felt the differences between Britain and the homelands were:

These are very odd people I thought. They paint their buildings black. Well I wasn't to know it was soot, was I?[4]

Agnes Dupont, however, felt that:

It was not such a disappointment to me, as I had always wanted to leave down there, and our ship also had a big party. I was so glad that I did not notice the coldness and the surroundings in Birmingham that were industrial and smoggy. The funny thing was that if I had seen something like 'Halfwaytree' (St. Kitts) then I would have been very upset as I did not want to be reminded of back home.

In contrast, some immigrants were unnerved by the sheer scale of their adopted country. Edgar Edmead remembers:

You have to understand what it was like for us back then. I could not believe the size of the city and all of the people. I recall wondering that most of the football matches

*played in Birmingham each had an
attendance that was more than the
population of my island back home.*

The arrival of Caribbean immigrants into
Great Britain was met with a mixture of
responses from both the government and
residents. The Colonial Secretary Creech
Jones remarked that, "these people have
British passports, and they must be
allowed to land.....There's nothing to
worry about, because they won't last one
winter in England."[5] As Braithwaite
points out, so-called British tolerance was
about to be put to the test:

*These same British, who had colonised
nearly three quarters of the world, and
acquired a reputation for tolerance and
justice in these territories, were suddenly
finding that this reputation was being tested
where they least welcomed such testing; on
their own doorstep.*[6]

The position of West Indian immigrants
exhibited many inequalities by
comparison to their British counterparts
particularly in relation to housing and
employment. Many believed that their
status as British subjects would ensure
that the indigenous population would
accept them, yet this was far from being
the case:

The settlers from the West Indies found a

Wedding of John and Bernice Walters, Aston 1958

*society remarkably unprepared for their
incorporation into its elaborate class and
cultural networks.*[7]

Unfortunately, cultural and social
differences, together with prejudice and
misunderstandings contributed to a
complexity of inter-communal
relationships, particularly in the inner
cities:

*Even when no slight was intended, let
alone hostility expressed, the contrast
between traditional British reticence and
the easy friendliness which they (the West
Indians) were accustomed to in their
homelands was disconcerting.*[8]

Many West Indians felt that they were
treated like colonial inferiors. Recalling
his first impressions of Great Britain,
John Walters remarks:

I must say that some English people were very helpful and concerned for our welfare. At least that is the way I read their questions: "Do you feel the cold much?" was always one of the questions that I was asked. The funny thing is that the weather was not all that we found cold about England.

Prejudice, however, was not exclusive to any one racial group and some newcomers were not entirely surprised by the cold reception which they encountered. To explain this notion it is helpful to briefly examine the traditions of the West Indies. The region, in its complete entirety, is made up of a multitude of islands both large and small with each possessing its own individual and varying culture and values including musical tastes and dialect. The idea of belonging, 'Nation' and 'Mother Country' was an important ethos to most West Indians. Despite a tradition of tolerance, which was borne out of a slave centred colonial past, the West Indies still had its own caste system. Black people with clear complexions tended to gain access to better jobs and positions in society. Differential treatment towards people from other islands still occurred. George Henry confirms this:

It did not surprise me when I noticed how the people used to treat us, and think bad

things about us, when we first came here. That is why I made sure that I attempted to keep myself to myself. No one likes foreigners coming to their place of birth to live. Think of the way we in St. Kitts used to treat the Montserrations (natives of Montserrat, a smaller island). We used to give them hell, their women could never get gainful employment. Do not listen to black people who say that they were surprised at the reactions of the British to their being here.

George Henry, 1956

References

(1)   This is is a very contentious point and I had great difficulty in obtaining a clear directive on this issue. Memories are long with most people and their reasons for changing their surnames possibly held bad memories of which the name change was meant to obliterate. Caution was uppermost when I attempted to discuss this topic and none of the female interviewees would speak on the subject.
(2)   Hunt, J. Article. 'Race Relations in Britain: The Decisive Decade' in Patterns of Prejudice. Vol 1. No.6 Nov/Dec. (1967)
(3)   Banton, M. Article. 'The Changing Position of the Negro in Britain'. Phylon 14 (1953) p.82
(4)   Western, J. Passage to England Barbadian Londoners Speak of Home. (1992) p.56
(5)   Hennessy, P. Ibid. p.440
(6)   Braithwaite, E. R. Reluctant Neighbours (1972) p.81
(7)   Rich, P. Propero's Return. (1994) p.153
(8)   Segal, R. The Black Diaspora (1995) p.277

HOUSING AND EMPLOYMENT

Much of the conflict which surrounded the initial relationships between the indigenous population and Caribbean immigrants first materialised because of the pre-conceived image most British people already had of West Indians. This was the result of misconstrued propaganda and a general feeling of xenophobia. It is also important to recognise that the often stereotypical image which many British people had of West Indians was severely compounded by the poor and squalid conditions which these same West Indians were forced into after their arrival in Great Britain. Decent housing and employment were very difficult to find and new arrivals often ended up grouped together in the rundown inner cities, where not only were living conditions very poor but they also often found themselves the objects of exploitation.

Samuel 'Sonny' Philips (left) with 'Old Jack' and Noran Beaupierre (Nevis) in a pub in Bradford Street, Digbeth 1957

The Labour government's Housing Acts of 1946 and 1949 did nothing to protect prospective immigrant lodgers against the Rachmanism of the 1950s or the 'No Blacks, No Irish, No Dogs' signs which were frequently displayed by many landlords particularly during the post war era.

Samuel 'Sonny' Phillips recounts his first experience of lodging, when he arrived in Birmingham:

I first lodged with an Asian man who had an English girlfriend. There were two double beds and four of us would sleep in them at night and four on the day, so the beds were never unused. They were crafty people. On a Saturday she would make sure she got a full stamp dividend off the Co-Operative man for the milk that she ordered for us. Even though she gave us a fresh egg now and then, I did not study her and the Asian landlord, this was because I could not trust them.

Many West Indians encountered varied experiences when they initially attempted to secure lodgings for themselves. This is illustrated when considering the comments of Edgar and Ena Edmead. Edgar Edmead recalls:

A Jamaican man, William Grant, had a house at number twenty eight Morden Road, Stechford, in Birmingham. Eight of us slept in one bedroom there on my first night in England. Apart from the very few West Indians, only Polish people and Asians would even talk to you about a room. I am not sure about how Grant purchased the house, maybe he was part of a 'pardner hand', but I never asked him. I trusted Grant, he helped us out, he charged me one pound two shillings and sixpence for the bed a week.

Edgar Edmead celebrating moving to his new house, Small Heath 1957

Ena Edmead offers a contrasting view to that of her husband:

When I moved to Stechford I had a room in Frederick Road, which was luxurious compared to Edgar Edmead's room. At least we had an electric meter and paraffin lamps. In Edgar's lodgings they had to get cardboard and wooden boxes from the greengrocer to build a fire with. The only problem that I had was that when I put my penny or sixpence in the meter a Jamaican woman from across the way would attempt to use the hot water or to use the gas as everything was metered. This led to a lot of noise in the lodging.

Landlords such as William Grant, who could afford to owner-occupy were a rarity, particularly when they did not reside in the port areas of the country where links between West Indians were more established. The 'pardner hand' that Edgar Edmead speaks of was a crude way of saving money amongst many groups of West Indians. Each week the members would contribute a set amount of money into a kitty, which was then given to one of the group to secure what he or she wanted to purchase. Then as the hand went around each member would be the recipient of the money when it was his or her turn. Sadly prospective house purchasers often found themselves either isolated from family and friends or faced with vendor's inflated house prices to prevent them devaluing the properties around them. Ultimately the social segregation of most immigrants, particularly in relation to housing, only succeeded in worsening their already dire position as J. Rex points out:

The West Indian tenant now finds himself living in the 'twilight zone' of the city, a life with a style and a stink of its own. It is not the life of the slums. Slums have a place in the thinking of the Welfare State, twilight zones have not.[1]

Delatris and Hazel Thomas, Blackpool 1956

Although many immigrants lived in squalid conditions they still retained their high standards of hygiene and their personal pride was not forsaken:

Let me tell you a story about bread young man. When I first came to this country I was shocked to see that the white people let the bread man leave the bread on their doorstep without any covering. When he asked us in our lodgings would we like to order some bread we told him yes but that he must wrap it up in a cloth, or paper. So it still gets to me when we hear that the white people thought of us as dirty.[2]

To reinforce this point one only has to examine the household traditions of many West Indian families. A huge emphasis was and still is placed on the front room, which was seen as the most significant room in the house. It was treated in an almost 'shrine like' manner and was where the best furniture was placed. It also contained the drinks cabinet, the best family pictures, the souvenirs of seaside trips of places that had been visited, or given as gifts by friends. The room was also seen as a place of sanctuary, where the father or mother could gather their thoughts after a hard day's work in an often hostile world. It was a room where children were forbidden except during weddings, funerals and festivals such as Christmas day when they would take over the activities under the tree.

The wedding reception of Samuel 'Sonny' and Berdy Philips at a pub in Albert Road, Aston 1958. Berdy Philips died tragically when the 'Christina' travelling between St. Kitts and Nevis capsized with the loss of over a hundred lives in 1970.

The issue of employment also raised many serious concerns for Caribbean immigrants. These related to how badly they were being discriminated against in this particular sphere. An assessment of the employment issue illustrates that where work was available it was limited to certain occupations. The presence of

the ubiquitous 'No Coloureds' notices in Labour Exchanges contributed to the presence of a colour bar in Great Britain during the 1950s. The Times newspaper reported that:

Officials of the TGWU in Birmingham have invited a Colonial Office spokesman, who is a Jamaican, to meet Birmingham Corporation bus workers in an attempt to persuade them to accept coloured workers for platform duties.....The services of coloured men and women had been neglected although there were 860 vacancies for conductors, it is probably the worst case of the colour bar in the country.[3]

This was obviously a clear failure of the Ministry of Labour, who were responsible for setting up the Labour Exchanges, and it also casts a doubt on their claim that they were unaware of such policies and notices.

On arriving in Britain many immigrants felt that there was a policy of double standards in existence which ensured that skilled workers, particularly those needed by the new national bodies such as the NHS, were given every assistance in gaining employment. Samuel Grant recalls:

My mother, she is now dead, showed me her documentation from her journey over.

On it there were concise instructions on how to get from the port (Southampton) to London, and then to Birmingham. She told me that it was because she told them that she had trained as a nurse that they treated her quite well. All of her untrained friends had to make their own arrangements to get over here.

Frederick Dorsett taken before his departure for England in 1958. Frederick was a painter and decorator in Guyana.

Others, however, who had trained as teachers in the West Indies, found that their qualifications did not meet British criteria and so had to do menial work.[4] West Indians who had travelled over in

the 1950s and who were more qualified than their indigenous peers frequently encountered this policy:

I was an oddity. A black man with a Masters degree and cultured speech who'd flown spitfires during the war applying for work at their level. On several occasions the interview hardly touched on my technical qualifications.[5]

Many orthodox accounts of these years also fail to mention that many immigrants had left with skills that could help rather than hold back the economy: 'Of the men who came here a mere thirteen per cent had no skills, of the women, only five per cent. In fact, one in four of the men and half of the women were non-manual workers'.[6]

Some critics, such as Ceri Peach, have consistently argued that there developed a cycle of immigration from the West Indies which fitted well with the number of vacancies in Great Britain during the 1950s.[7] Some immigrants found securing employment a difficult task and felt that they were in a 'no win' situation as they were penalised for being both over-skilled and under-skilled. Hazel Thomas remembers:

The Labour exchange sent me to a factory called Oriental Tubes in Church Street

West Bromwich. I had only been in England for two weeks. A woman who met me there told me that as I had no experience of the press machinery I could not be considered for employment. I persevered and asked to be shown around and I looked at how the people worked the presses. Then I asked a foreman named Frankie for a trial on the press and I was so good that he did not believe that I had never worked on one before. I secured that job and subsequently brought many other West Indian people to the factory for work.

Others, however, found life in the factory a frustrating experience, as Ena Edmead states:

It makes me angry when I think back. My sister told them she was a nurse and they gave her every possible assistance. I found a job on piece-rate in a factory making components for cars. It was at the Wilmot Breedon plant at Kings Road, Hay Mills, Birmingham. Within two weeks I had caught my finger in one of the machines unaccustomed as I was to them. When I returned to work I received half pay because I had to work one handed.

British employers often took advantage of immigrant workers. Many West Indian workers found themselves forced into cheap labour at local factories in order to survive where they were often under-paid in comparison to their fellow white workers. Linford Brock's story illustrates this:

A white lad I teamed up with called Dave was with me in a pub and informed me that the firm were paying me short money. The following week I asked the foreman about it and told him that I had found Dave's wage slip and noticed that he was getting nine pounds as against my seven pounds ten shillings. He said that he would sort it out. The next thing I heard was that Dave had been sacked.

References

(1) Rex, J. Article. 'Social Segregation of the Immigrants in British Cities' in Political Quartley. No.39 (1968). Social segregation of immigrants often meant that families were split up. West Indian women were often not allowed to live with their husbands or men friends as this would upset the male/female balance of the rooming system. Single sex rooms were encouraged because they meant more money. Mr Edmead was separated from his partner Ena who lived at a room in West Bromwich some fifteen miles away. Partners, however, could live in the same room with a close relative also in occupation. If for example a relative was due to travel to England a reserve price was put on the newcomer's bed until they arrived.
(2) Story first told to me by a Jamaican driver on a building site in Nechells, Birmingham, 1982. Later this was corroborated by Mr Edmead and Mr Robert Mitcham (Arrival 1956) on Christmas Day 1994
(3) The Times Feb 9th (1954) p.3
(4) Hiro, D. Black British, White British. (1991) p.16
(5) Braithwaite, E. R. Reluctant Neighbours . Ibid p.42
(6) Fryer, P. Staying Power: The History of Black People in Britain. (1984) p374
(7) Gorz, A. Article. 'The role of Immigrant Labour' in New Left Review No.61. (1970) p.31

THE POLITICAL ANGLE

The Dyche Collection, Birmingham Central Library

The topic of immigration, particularly when it relates to political and economic factors, often leads to conflicting opinions. Holmes, for example, argues that: 'whatever qualities were present among the workers drawn from the Caribbean.....their net addition to population, even if this could not be gauged with a fine accuracy, was hardly of sufficient size to exert a significant impact on the economy.'[1] Some writers, however, such as Andrew Roberts blame immigration for the future economic ills

of the nation. With hindsight, he states that: 'at a time when Britain desperately needed to move from labour to capital intensive structures immigration held her back.'[2]

Any analysis of the immigration debates of the 1950s clearly illustrates that there was government concern surrounding the issue, but this was also clouded with a certain amount of confusion. Solomos points out that: 'contrary to the arguments of some scholars it seems quite inadequate to see this period as an age of innocence and lack of concern about black immigration into the United Kingdom.'[3] What does emerge from an analysis of this period is that immigration was somewhat conveniently put onto the sidelines of the political arena, without being totally ignored. Political debates, particularly between 1948 and 1962, demonstrate that government administrations from Attlee to Macmillan did not formulate a successful policy to deal with the problems of immigration, and so as Braithwaite deduced: 'successive British governments either blithely ignored the continuing racial strife or treated it with benign neglect.'[4]

A review of the Divisive Decade illustrates that immigration caused some governmental concern, particularly in relation to politics and economics. After the Second World War Great Britain, like many other developed Western democracies, was caught up on a wave of idealism. An ethos of justice and equal opportunity for all was promoted, particularly after the downfall of Nazi Fascism. Great Britain, as the titular head of the Commonwealth, could not afford to be seen as putting a curb on Negro immigration. As Britain was busy criticising policies of racial separation in both South Africa and the United States of America, any government legislation

against immigration would ultimately be seen as an outright act of hypocrisy:

Much of the political thinking in the Westminster-Whitehall Centre was thoroughly attuned to race in the post-war years, and as the centre of an emerging Commonwealth of Nations, the British government could not afford to be subject to charges of racial discrimination.[5]

Delatris Thomas 1956

The quandary which British policy makers found themselves in was deepened by the fact that 'until 1962 Britain was alone amongst (white) Commonwealth countries in freely admitting Commonwealth citizens without control of any kind.'[6]

Grahm Benny and friend, New John Street, Newtown 1950

What emerges from this period is a confused and unsuccessful attempt on behalf of the 'Mother Country' to discourage immigration without appearing overtly discriminatory. Government policies on immigration appeared to be justified because many people believed that immigration could cause economic problems. Thus, after the hostilities of the Second World War, there was an attempt to invest British capital into the Caribbean region to prevent the need for further West Indian immigration. This, however, was clearly unsuccessful mainly because of the previous lack of British investment which had virtually destroyed the West Indian economy. Further attempts by the British government to control the price of sugar also failed. The economic difficulties which Britain found itself in were revealed by their economic deficit of 1947. Their attempts at creating a Federation of the West Indies, with stronger economic links between the islands was also doomed to failure:

All economic relations in an empire flow from colony to centre and back. There is almost no exchange in an economic sense between the different colonies themselves even when they form part of a region, as is the case with the West Indian islands.[7]

Britain's weak economic position meant that it could not secure the investment that was needed to maintain its prior position in the West Indies.

Economic factors were not solely responsible for influencing governmental policy on immigration. It could even be argued that they only served to mask the more controversial concerns which many politicians had in relation to the social implications of immigration. The race debate was intricate and deeply ingrained in traditional British values. Solomos states that:

It is important to note, however, that these debates were not purely about the supposed characteristics of black migrants. They were also about the effect of black immigration on the racial character of the British people and the national identity. [8]

It would seem that the agendas of political debates during the 1950s were being set by a group of politicians who wished to put a stop to immigration. This is illustrated by the political reactions which emerged during attempts at introducing anti-discriminatory legislation. The Bills of 1950, 1953 and 1956 by Reginald Sorenson and Fenner Brockway were talked out of parliament as, after 1951, the Conservative administration sought to put forward its own agenda in the debate:

Since the 1950s a small handful of Conservative backbench MPs had regularly asked parliamentary questions on the issue of coloured immigration, to their front bench colleagues, and had argued the case for immigration control based on the spurious need to combat disease and criminality. [9]

The political debate was charged with various alarmist concepts, whereby West Indian immigrants were blamed for everything from the increase in sexually transmitted diseases to the increase in fights involving knives: 'race was thus fixed in a matrix between the imagery of squalor and that of sordid sexuality'. [10]

The impact which immigration had upon the social and political policies of the time should not be underestimated:

In building its strong case for immigration control the state undertook nothing less than a populist political project which both reconstructed an image of a national community that was homogeneous in its whiteness and racialized culture, and defended it from the allegedly corrosive influence of groups whose skin colour debarred them from belonging. [11]

References

(1) Holmes, C. John Bull's Island (1988) pp.233-234
(2) Roberts, A. Ibid. p.218
(3) Solomos, J. Race and Racism in Contemporary Britain (1989) p.45
(4) Braithwaite, E. R. Writing in Empire Windrush Fifty Years of Writing About Black Britain (1998)
(5) Rich, P. Ibid. p.168
(6) Aspect of Britain. (1993) p.9
(7) Manley, M. (1988) History of West Indies Cricket. p.123
(8) Solomos, J. Ibid. p.47
(9) Saggar, S. (1992) Race and Politics in Britain. p.69
(10) Gilroy, P. (1993) There Ain't No Black in the Union Jack. p.80.
(11) Carter, Harris and Joshi. Writing in Inside Babylon. (1993) p.69.

RACIAL VIOLENCE

Traditional accounts of the period claim an interim of harmonious race relations and ignore an evident undercurrent of hostility and violence. Franklin Pencheon's experience substantiates this point:

The Dyche Collection, Birmingham Central Library

Forget those riots at the end of the 1950s. Violence towards black people was always happening and was not just from one set of people. I learned my lesson very early. I was at a get-together, you could not even call it a party, somewhere in Winson Green

or Handsworth. It was just after I arrived in 1955. Sure enough the police arrived shouting and hitting the front door hard. They were trying to get the occupier, a Jamaican man, to open it. "What do you want", he asked them. "Open the door or we will break it down", they shouted. "Break down the door then", he said, "It is not my door, anyway, it belongs to Birmingham Corporation." Therefore I learned that the police were not necessarily going to look after us. I mean on that night they had no cause to be there. If you were dead silent with them and they did not think you were scared then they would leave you alone.

The climatic riots of 1958 were the end result of many previous sporadic outbreaks of racial violence, which ultimately demonstrate that the Divisive Decade was a continuous, unfragmented period in modern British history which possessed its own complexities. The occurrence of racism was exacerbated by the phenomenon of 'poor whites' - working class people who could not afford to join the hasty exodus from inner city areas in response to the arrival of black immigrants. The potential friction between these two communities was sometimes exploited cynically by politicians: 'it is significant, however, that the solutions considered to this problem were to stop black immigration rather than to combat white racism.'[1]

The Dyche Collection, Birmingham Central Library

An earlier incident of violence in August 1948 at a hostel near Birmingham between Poles and Jamaicans was thought to have erupted over a ridiculous argument about which people had more right to be in the nation. An article in The Times reported that, 'where Poles and coloured West Indian workers lived in the same hostel there were occasional disputes over the relative dignitaries of British Citizenship and the possession of a white skin.'[2] Although these arguments may appear to have been manifestations of male bravado, they did reveal an obvious problem for West Indian immigrants:

White newcomers...had alternatives: they could, for example, fade into the rest of the population and in time lose the more obvious marks of foreignness such as accent. Dark-skinned migrants, however, could not get rid of their colour, even if they wanted to.[3]

An Irish former soldier John 'Jack' White reinforces this point of view:

It was easy for us. All we had to do was keep our mouths shut. When you think about it the black people had no chance as the English took them at face value a lot of the time, without even trying to get to know them.

Political motivation, particularly that initiated by Oswald Mosley, also incited some of the violence which occurred during the decade:

Officials of the British Caribbean Welfare Service suggested that in West London the rioters had been deliberately incited to violence. The officials alleged that attacks on coloured people had begun after the Union Movement (formerly the British Union of Fascists) led by Sir Oswald Mosley had distributed leaflets in the Notting Hill area.[4]

The Jamaican conscript Baron Baker states:

The Dyche Collection, Birmingham Central Library

Mosley tried to stir up a conflict between the blacks and the whites because his aim was to drive the blacks from North Kensington, to drive them from the shores of England. I wasn't for that because I came over here to fight for the Mother Country.[5]

Overt fascism was not just confined to London. Brown-shirted Mosley fascists also held rallies in Handsworth park at the beginning of the 1960s.

The lack of a government policy in

relation to immigration also contributed to the violence which occurred. As Layton-Henry points out:

The failure of central government to provide local authorities with additional funds to alleviate the shortage of housing and accommodation in areas of immigrant settlement was a contributing factor to inter-racial hostility.[6]

Yet had this taken place there would have been a risk of white residents arguing that the newcomers were attaining preferential treatment.

Throughout this period traditional British values of tolerance and understanding were being questioned and undermined. Many immigrants came to realise that the 'Mother Country' was not a place where they would be welcome or belong:

Elderly West Indians were the most severely affected...they had venerated the image of the Mother Country even more strongly than their children, so they were even more shattered when it turned out to be an illusion.[7]

The violence, however, did have a positive effect on the West Indian community. The usual inter-island rivalry that had always been a part of the culture of the

West Indies was replaced by a new spirit of togetherness:

The riots for the first time helped to ease the divisions between Jamaicans, Trinidadians, Barbadians and others and allowed organisations such as the West Indian Standing Conference (1958) to come into being. [8]

A bond of solidarity amongst fellow immigrants emerged as blacks united against the violence and began to defend each other as a whole community. Western reinforces this significant historical change:

The Dyche Collection, Birmingham Central Library

At the same time as whites were descending on Notting Hill to join in the affray, black people were doing likewise...The Jamaicans bore the brunt of the fighting in Notting Hill - they fought back fiercely. A message that is clearly broadcast here is that inter-island rivalries were buried when white hostility was staring one in the face. [9]

The ineffectiveness of a governmental representative team which was sent over from the Caribbean to tour certain areas of Great Britain after the violence of 1958, also promoted further unity amongst the West Indian Community. It reinforced the feeling that it was now in their own interests to look to each other and not across the ocean for their survival in this new and challenging society:

Racial discrimination in Britain was not an overnight phenomenon, and it was pitiable that there still could be found no effective representative group of West Indians who could honestly claim the right to speak or act on behalf of the rank and file in a time of crisis... Many of them were easily and fluently articulate or otherwise gifted; they should put some of those talents to work to help raise the standards of those less equipped than themselves. [10]

Any idyllic thoughts that some West Indians may have harboured about their place in British society quickly disappeared. Yet, although solidarity in a cruel environment was beneficial, the negative effect was that it also led to further segregation of the different races, as, 'gradually the West Indians began to set up their own clubs and welfare associations, or met in barber shops and cafes... as they were wont to do back home'.[11]

The Dyche Collection, Birmingham Central Library

Before 1958 there was a deep suspicion amongst ordinary West Indians of their fellow middle class immigrants. So called 'ordinary' black people seemed to have an aversion to listening to the good advice of their more knowledgeable peers. Braithwaite writes:

I had to prove myself to them. Suspecting and expecting betrayal from one of their own kind, they made my work extremely difficult. Deliberately they would be late for appointments at my office, or be absent from home when I was expected to call.[12]

Sadly for some the bonds of solidarity were not enough to make them stay, and so they took the ultimate step of returning to their place of origin. Clearly, in their view, Harold Macmillan's 'never had it so good' nation had failed them. Once they had returned they were forced to face the ridicule of those who always argued that the British were only using West Indian labour for their own ends. This must have been a galling experience for them considering the sacrifices that many West Indian families had originally made to send the family member to Great Britain in the first place.

References

(1) Kushner, T. Writing in 20th Century Britain. (1994) p.414
(2) The Times. Article. Foreign Workers in Britain May 21st (1951)
(3) Ramdin, R. (1987) The Making of the Black Working Class in Britain. p.189
(4) Taken from Keesings Contermporary Archives. Vol.1. (1957-1958) p.16428
(5) Baker, Baron. Writing in, Humphries and Gordon, P. (1994) Forbidden Britain Our Secret Past. p.110
(6) Layton-Henry, Z. (1984) The Politics of Race in Britain. p.35.
(7) Pilkington, E. (1988) Beyond Mother Country, West Indians and the Notting Hill Riots. p.140.
(8) Kushner, T. Writing in Johnson, P. Ibid. p.145
(9) Western, J. (1992) Passage to England, Barbadian Londoners Speak of Home. p.64
(10) Braithwaite, E. R. (1962) Paid Servant. p.137
(11) Sivanandan, A. Article. From Resistance to Rebellion Asian and Afro-Caribbean Struggles in Britain. In Race and Class. Vol.23. (1981-1982) p.113
(12) Braithwaite, E.R. (1972) Reluctant Neighbours. p.83

INDIGENOUS ATTITUDES
AND THE MEDIA

Andy Hamilton and his band, The Dyche Collection, Birmingham Central Library

Caribbean immigrants arrived into an atmosphere of prejudice in Britain; it was not a neutral ideological void. Patterson suggests that:

The attitude expressed in the familiar sentence, 'there's a stranger let's heave half a brick at him' is no new one in England. It has been motivated in part by a general xenophobia against people of other religions and cultures, but by more specific economic jealousies and apprehensions.[1]

The onset of slavery and colonisation particularly during the sixteenth and seventeenth century had a major effect on the shaping of indigenous attitudes during subsequent years, as James Walvin points out:

While it would be untrue to say that the history of blacks in Britain is uniform and has an unbroken thread since the seventeenth century, it is indisputable that blacks have been a feature of English society and history for centuries. It is in the main, an unhappy story, for throughout much of the period black/white relations were shaped by the experience of slavery and, later by imperial domination. [2]

The Dyche Collection, Birmingham Central Library

Throughout these centuries both slavery and colonisation were justified by a popular and widely accepted philosophy which argued that black people were both physically and mentally inferior to whites. This concept was carried forward into the nineteenth century and was particularly encouraged by the Victorians who:

Disliked the physical appearance of black skin and further found the nakedness of Africans repulsive. In addition, they saw blacks as lazy, superstitious, dishonest and

sexually promiscuous. [3]

As a result of these beliefs, it is no surprise that most Britons, particularly during the 1950s still held the old prejudiced view that a black person was akin to the:

Familiar caricature in books and films, a shiftless indolent character, living either in a primitive mud hut or in the more deplorable shanty town, and meeting all life's problems with a flashing smile, a sinuous dance and a drum-assisted song. [4]

Many West Indian immigrants who had settled in England during and after World War One had suffered at the hands of white racists. The Times reported the occurrence of rioting in several cities throughout Great Britain. Indigenous attitudes during the 1950s were strengthened by lurid tales which had emerged in inter-war Britain, detailing the escapades of immigrants. One involved the Oriental drug dealer 'Brilliant Chang'. Another related to the black Jamaican Norman Manning who was alleged to have organised a white slave trade of prostitution. Scotland Yard went so far as to dub Manning 'the most dangerous man in London'. The Pathe newsreel of the Trinidadian calypso artist 'Lord Kitchener' espousing the greatness of London Town from the bows of the

Empire Windrush did nothing to counteract the image that many white Britons already had of West Indians.

A factor which also reinforced indigenous attitudes was a debate which prevailed during the 1950s, questioning the sexual behaviour of some West Indian men. This debate can be traced from the Victorian belief that black people were more inclined to be sexually promiscuous. Meryck Edwards who arrived in Great Britain in 1957 counteracts this argument:

Meryck Edwards' Jamaican Driving Licence, 1955

They were always on about how certain black men behaved back then, but they could not see it. Of course some black men were very active sexually with white women, with no intention of settling down with them, but surely the women's behaviour was just as bad. Their behaviour was just the same as the British had behaved in the West Indies centuries before. Their slave systems did not encourage marriage so did their method of control affect the West Indian mentality? The 1950s did not surprise me, the whites still thought they owned you, and were put out if a black man went with their women.

Caribbean immigrants were accustomed to co-existing peacefully with people from different races, particularly because the islands were populated by more than one racial group. They found the negative attitudes and reactions of the host nation both confusing and disturbing, especially as Britain was promoting itself as a tolerant and liberal nation. George Henry suggests:

I do not believe that they really came to terms with all of it. We were waiting by the gates of the factory one morning when one of the foremen looked over at us and saw a white man from Jamaica standing with us. He shook his head and said, 'He walks like them, talks like them, and hangs around with them, but he looks like us!

Although many West Indians were disturbed by the overt racism which they encountered on a daily basis and were shocked by the way they were treated, some actually managed to turn such situations to their own advantage, as Linford Brock humorously recalls:

I quickly realised that the white conductors on my bus journey to and from the city were reluctant to take my fare. So each evening I would make sure that I boarded a bus which had a white man on the platform. Those extra pennies bought me an extra beer at the weekend.

Enos Clarke, 1961

The treatment of white West Indian immigrants, which was certainly different to that of their fellow black West Indian counterparts, illustrates the hypocrisy behind a lot of indigenous attitudes. Enos Clarke's (a very clear looking West Indian) experience illustrates this:

Of course my treatment was different to that of the black West Indians that came over. I was at a dance at the Tower Ballroom in Edgbaston with a lot of Jamaican friends. I was pleased to be there. The dance was playing West Indian music and a lot of black people were present. I was in the toilet when a flustered looking white man came up to me and said, 'There's a lot of them in here tonight?' 'Yes there's a lot of them in here tonight', I answered, trying not to laugh at his concern. 'Do you think we'll be alright?' he asked. 'Yes I think we will be okay, they are not as bad as people think you know', I replied.

Racial prejudice, however, was not always prevalent amongst all British residents and some were well aware of the experiences of the immigrants. John 'Jack' White recalls:

I was stationed at Up Park Camp military base in Kingston, Jamaica, from 1947 to 1949. I was not pleased about going there because after fighting on the river Elbe, and seeing out the war my battalion, the Royal Ulster Rifles, were told we could have some leave after our stint in Palestine. Two weeks later we were sent to Jamaica. The locals treated us well and we knew that many West Indians had fought well for the Allies. Where I think a lot of the immigration reaction went wrong was that the British man in the street was not aware of these facts.

The British media also unwittingly played a part in both misunderstanding West Indians and reinforcing stereotypes of them. The Times reported: 'they are said not to like working in high temperatures, rather surprisingly, and some managers think the explanation is to be found in their inferior physique.' The report seems to contradict itself, inferring that the immigrants should be able to work in high temperatures, because of their tropical backgrounds, but because of their inferior physical attributes they do not appear to be producing their quota. No mention was made, however, of the type of work that the immigrants were doing, or the fact that it might have been new or monotonous to them, particularly as many of these people were from rural backgrounds. The report continues:

(In the workplace), almost without exception they get on excellently with white workers, but they have been known to quarrel amongst themselves on what might be called national lines. Immigrants from the Leeward Islands, for example, who seem to have the highest reputation of them as workmen, do not always work easily in harness with Jamaicans.[5]

The fact that Leeward Islanders did not work well with Jamaicans is easy to explain. Their island mentalities would make them reticent towards each other, just as white people would probably have a hidden reluctance if they were to work beside someone from a different region or nationality. Also, it would be natural for people who are always in conversation at the workplace to find areas of disagreement on very banal matters. This would have been the case with West Indians as with any other set of workers. The Times did not investigate how many white workers argued about football matches, or what their favourite film was in order to balance the argument. The fact that the immigrants appeared to get on well with indigenous workers also begs the question of how deeply they got to know the other. Wilfred Greaves remembers:

Work was not too bad. In fact it was quite easy. This was because we may have been cautious of who we spoke with. I soon teamed up with Eddie Edmead, who is my brother-in-law, and another Bajan, Victor

Blackman. Of course we would speak and socialise with the English people but you knew that you felt more secure with those who were like you.

Wilfred Greaves, Jerome Studios, Union Street 1956

West Indians have a tradition of using very natural and literal nicknames for their friends and colleagues and many West Indian immigrants, particularly within the workplace, often continued this tradition. Some examples of these names include, 'Big Finger Jones', a worker with enormous fingers, 'Motion', a man with a slow motion walk and 'Peter

Waterman', because he worked as a water dispenser to workers in the sugar cane fields. These nicknames were often used to show familiarity and solidarity between friends and, as illustrated, were usually personalised and very descriptive. They were never, however, meant to be offensive. Enos Clarke recalls how some of his fellow white workers had noticed this behaviour and so decided to give him his own nickname:

I was working at I.M.I. in Witton and white people there called me 'Omo' after the washing powder. What struck me as odd was the fact that I was as white as they were, so why was everybody else not called 'Omo' or some other nickname. The reason they saw a difference in me was that I too was an immigrant and they, in their small minds, needed to acknowledge this difference.

It would be unfair to be totally critical of the media of the 1950s. It did attempt various initiatives to bring home the problems that many immigrants were facing in Great Britain at the time. Some of these, however, were a little misguided: 'public concern at such developments was revealed in the Pathe newsreel "Our Jamaican Problem" in 1955, and a BBC Panorama programme of 1956 which engaged in a survey of racial discrimination and disadvantage.'[6] The

Charles Edmeade, Lacey's Studios, Small Heath 1960. Charles was known for a time as 'Peter Waterman'.

I was pleased to meet an English man at work when I came over called Ted. Ted told me that he was well read and he used the libraries frequently. He asked me which islands I was from and I told him the Leewards. 'Yes I know St. Kitts, Antigua, Nevis...' One day it was snowing, one of the first I had ever seen and Ted shouted to me 'Gosh son it's cold - when are you going to win the pools and take me back to Jamaica with you!'

Panorama documentary about the presence of a colour bar was well received by all apart from the employers that it pinpointed. A more contentious issue was that although the Pathe newsreel 'Our Jamaican Problem' highlighted the difficulties that many West Indians were having in inner London and offered various solutions to these problems, such as inter-racial dances, West Indians felt that the title of the newsreel inferred that all immigrants from the West Indies were from Jamaica. This generalisation is one that has always proved to be a contentious issue with West Indians. Samuel 'Sonny' Philips highlights this problem:

Although the examples above largely portray the media as actively promoting a negative image of West Indian immigrants, some newspapers did attempt to educate the British public about the situation. An article appeared in the Daily Mirror with the headline 'Introducing to you...The Boys from Jamaica.' This article attempted to dispel the common misconception that West Indians were all wasters, criminals or heathens, who were only interested in stealing women, houses and jobs from white people.[7]

What emerges from this assessment of indigenous attitudes during the 1950s is that most Britons held a paradoxical view of West Indian immigrants:

They took our jobs, but they were on national assistance. They were lazy but they also worked too hard. They were after our women but they did not mix.[8]

Doris and Graham Bennie, New John Street, Newtown 1949

Stereotyping had become a complex affair whereby positive images of black people were included alongside negative ones.

Indeed...in certain fields of English cultural life, such as sport, the entertainment world, and in philanthropic circles, colour has a positive rather than a negative value. This is largely because the expert sprinter, able musician, or eloquent platform speaker fits in with the popular stereotype of the Negro as athlete, entertainer, or poor black brother.[9]

It would seem that these positive images of black people were still formed from a stereotype based on an image that posed no threat to the indigenous population. Unfortunately the result was that,

generally, indigenous attitudes towards the West Indian immigrants still tended to be prejudiced.

References

(1) Patterson, S. Article. Immigrants and Employment. In Political Quarterly. No.39. (1968) p.54
(2) Walvin, J. Article. Blacks in Britain. In History Today. September (1981) p.39
(3) Panayi, P. Immigration, Ethnicity and Racism in Britain. 1815-1945 p.119 (1994)
(4) Braithwaite, E.R. To Sir With Love (1959) p.100
(5) The Times. Series., The West Indian Settlers 9th Nov. (1954) p.9
(6) Deakin, N. Article. The Politics of the Commonwealth Immigrants Bill. In Political Quarterly. Vol.39. (1968) p.259
(7) Daily Mirror 6th Sept (1958)
(8) Porter, D. Writing in From Blitz to Blair. Tiratsoo, N. (Ed) (1997). pp.117-118
(9) Little, K. Article. The Position of Coloured People in Britain. Phylon. 15. (1954) p.58

CONCLUSION

The term 'divisive' is defined as: 'tending to cause disagreement or dissension.'[1] When referring to the 'Divisive Decade' this definition is very apt. Disagreement is certainly associated with various aspects of this epoch. As discussed in the introduction to this book, many people often associate the prelude to this decade, and in particular the Windrush episode with the onset of Caribbean immigration. A closer examination of this period reveals this particular notion to be a myth. It is a myth, however, which has been widely accepted for generations and this has caused a great deal of disagreement between the West Indian community and those who tend to accept this version as the truth.

This more obvious instance of disagreement, however, is easily superseded by a more immediate and serious dispute, which this book has hopefully revealed. The emergence of various and often differing interpretations of the events, which took place during the 1950s, are the main sources of disagreement. For many years traditional historical accounts have led the thinking on this particular era. Yet, generally, these accounts only offered a one-dimensional interpretation of the period in question and, more importantly,

were often from the viewpoint of a white person. Inevitably these studies, which were at the time the only 'accepted' versions of history available, often failed to give any recognition to the individual black person's experience of life in Great Britain during this period. As Bullock points out, many historians in their attempt to find historical explanations often tend to 'study human beings collectively as members of groups, in which individual characteristics are submerged into the average.'[2] Even more disturbing, and a glaringly obvious oversight, is that they often omit the many and frequent instances of racial discrimination and prejudice which West Indian immigrants were faced with on a daily basis. It should also be noted that the accounts of those interviewed reveal that discrimination was a continuous process. Those who came to Great Britain in the 1960s also suffered the same humiliating and distressing treatment which was meted out on their counterparts in the previous two decades:

In considering the history of post-war immigration and its consequences, it is difficult to detect any automatic cycle of development, as a result of which immigrants have moved from an initial encounter with hostility, through a later stage of toleration, towards the nirvana of acceptance. Hostility sleeps lightly; it is soon awakened.[3]

Before the gradual emergence of alternative accounts, which were published in the early 1980s, these inherently biased historical accounts were the only sources available charting the West Indian experience during this time. The Caribbean experience was either understated or ignored. What emerges from an examination of this period is that Caribbean people had, and still have, a very different view of how they were treated during this period. Theirs is a perspective which significantly diverges from the generally more dominant version of events; which, in simple terms, tended to grossly oversimplify events and conveyed the idea that, apart from limited incidents of social unrest, immigrants were made welcome and life was generally satisfactory. As illustrated, this notion was also a myth, born out of a dominant white ideology.

Through reassessing the 'Divisive Decade' various issues of concern have surfaced. There was and still is a lot of confusion surrounding the reasons why West Indians came to Great Britain. It was not common knowledge that many immigrants had ventured to the 'Mother Country' in order to aid the war effort.

Although it was perceived that West Indians were taking jobs, what many people failed to realise was that West Indians had been directly recruited in their homelands. The most prominent of these recruitment policies were the National Health Service initiatives for nursing staff and the London Transport drive to recruit in Barbados in 1956. Aldith Warner recalls:

We had a big house in Forest Gate (East London) and were forever being contacted by London Transport to accept more lodgers to enable them to settle more easily into life in England. Many of the lodgers were given loans by the British for their travel, which they paid back out of their wages.

Many of these people were highly skilled workers in the West Indies, and some of them were in fact leaving well-paid jobs in order to offer their loyal assistance to Great Britain.

As revealed earlier the media played a large part in compounding the discrimination which West Indians encountered. They often created a wide variety of negative stereotypes which encouraged a general climate of racism. As a result West Indians found that prejudice filtered through to every aspect of their lives. It should be noted, however, that not all British residents were influenced by the media stereotyping of West Indians, as is illustrated by John 'Jack' White's numerous testaments. Yet it might be suggested that perhaps White was able to empathise more readily with the West Indian experience quite probably because he himself was classed as an immigrant, being Irish by birth.

Wilfred and Dora Greaves' wedding at St. Oswald's Church, Small Heath 1959. From left: Elyniss (daughter of Ena), Aldith Warner, Dora Greaves and Ena Edmead

The media, along with biased accounts from historians were not solely to blame for the discrimination which occurred during these years. Many West Indians

encountered prejudice and discrimination during and after World War One. The Times reported the occurrence of several riots in Britain between the black and white community in Liverpool, Canning Town, London, Cardiff and Newport. Racial prejudice was not a new experience.[4]

The discrimination which West Indian immigrants encountered during the 1950s, however, was not just a continuance of that which had occurred during the 1920s. Then the government passed legislation which meant that non-British seamen could no longer work on British ships. It was a symptom of an unequal power system which has been in existence for at least the last four hundred years; in fact since Britain began its almighty quest for mass colonisation.

Imperialism and the existence of racism were justified and strengthened by what Gordon and Newnham refer to as 'pseudo-scientific' concepts. In brief, black people were believed to be inferior to whites. This idea was advocated in the seventeenth century by the philosopher David Hume, who believed that: 'Africans, as descendants of Ham's son Canaan, were accused and doomed to servitude.' Gordon and Newnham suggest that these ideas were further developed in the nineteenth century, when many people believed that evolution and natural selection favoured the superiority of people of North European stock.[5] Ultimately, the prejudice which West Indians suffered during the 'Divisive Decade' was, in effect, only the symptom of a long-standing problem.

When reviewing the exodus to Britain of thousands of Caribbeans during the 'Divisive Decade' it becomes obvious how racism played a key part in the immigration process:

Instead of the Europeans occupying the colonies in order to take advantage of the labour power available, the indigenous inhabitants of the colonies have been brought to Europe to provide cheap labour there. If the Imperial situation has been thus reversed, the power structure remains exactly the same, something the racism of the right, which presents immigration as an alien wedge supposedly threatening the basis of English Culture and identity, chooses to ignore.[6]

The experiences of West Indian immigrants, particularly during the 1950s, illustrate that this particular phase of immigration was certainly complex. The traditional image of Britain as a modern, idealistic and tolerant nation is seriously questioned.

This idea is reinforced by Panias Panayi, a champion of studies which reinterpret this phase of British history and in particular those which question Britain's so called liberal traditions.

Although there is a national myth that Britain has always kept the door open to newcomers, the reality is that we have been as exclusive as most other societies.[7]

It is to be hoped that through exploring the experiences of the West Indian people who were interviewed we can begin the task of demystifying and, to a certain extent, demythologising not only various aspects of British history but also the process of Caribbean immigration. Those who offered their honest accounts can at least feel assured that they have played a vital role in challenging underlying racism. Their dignified and often painful memories highlight the racial prejudice which continues to permeate Britain's social structures.

References

(1) Collins Concise Dictionary, New Revised Edition. Glasgow, Harper Collins. p.37 (1995)
(2) Bullock, A. Hitler and Stalin, Parallel Lives. pp.1058-1059 (1993)
(3) Holmes, C. Writing in Gourvish, T and O'Day, A. (1991) Britain Since 1945. p.229
(4) The Times. 11th and 14th June (1919)
(5) Gordon, P and Newnham, A. Different Worlds, Racism and Discrimination in Britain. London, Runnymede Trust. p.1. (1986)
(6) Young, R. White Mythologies, Writing History and the West. pp.174-175 (1990)
(7) Panayi, P. Ibid. p.2

BIBLIOGRAPHY

Anwar, M. (1986) *Race and Politics. Participation of Ethnic Minorities.* London. Tavistock. ISBN: 0422798509

Bousquet, B and Douglas, C. (1991) *West Indian Women at War, British Racism in World War Two.* London. Lawrence and Wishart. ISBN: 085315743X

Braithwaite, E. R. (1962) *Paid Servant.* London. Bodley Head.

(1972) *Reluctant Neighbours.* Ibid. (1959) *To Sir With Love.*

Bullock, A. (1993) *Hitler and Stalin, Parallel Lives.* London. Fontana Press. ISBN: 0006861989

Fryer, P. (1984) *Staying Power: The History of Black People in Britain.* London. Pluto. ISBN: 0861047494

Gilroy, P. (1992) *There Ain't No Black in the Union Jack.* London. Routledge. ISBN: 0415084105

Gordon, P. and Newman, A. (1996) *Different Worlds, Racism and Discrimination in Britain.* London Runnymede Trust.

Gourvish, T and O'Day, A. (1991) *Britain Since 1945.* Basingstoke. Macmillan Education. ISBN: 0333491572

Grenville, J. (1994) *The Collins History of the World in the Twentieth Century.* London. Harper Collins. ISBN: 0002551691

Harris, C and James, W. (1993) *Inside Babylon.* London. Verso. ISBN: 0860914712

Hennessy, P. (1993) *Never Again: Britain 1945-1951.* London. Vintage. ISBN: 0099301210

Hiro, D. (1991) *Black British White British.* London. Grafton. ISBN: 02446136189

Holmes, C. (1988) *John Bull's Island.* Basingstoke. Macmillan. ISBN: 03332822094

Humphries, S. and Gordon, P. (1994) *Forbidden Britain Our Secret Past.* London. BBC Books. ISBN: 0563369744

Husband, C. (1982) *Race in Britain: Continuity and Change.* London. Hutchinson. ISBN: 0091469112

Johnson, P. (1994) *Twentieth Century Britain, Economic, Social and Cultural Change.* London. Longman. ISBN: 05822228174

Layton-Henry, Z. (1984) *The Politics of Race in Britain.* London. Allen & Unwin. ISBN: 00433230261

Lloyd, T. (1986) *Empire to Welfare State. English History 1906-1985.* Oxford. Oxford University Press. ISBN: 0198221355

Madgewick, Steeds and Williams. (1982) *Britain Since 1945.* London. Hutchinson. ISBN: 0091473713

Manley, M. (1988) *The History of West Indies Cricket.* London. Deutsch. ISBN: 0233982590

Morgan, K. (1990) *The People's Peace.* Oxford. Oxford University Press. ISBN: 0198227647

Nederveen Pieterse, J. (1992) *White on Black. Images of Africa and Blacks in Western Popular Culture.* London. Yale University Press. ISBN: 0300063113

Novick, P. (1990) *That Noble Dream*

Panayi, P. (1994) *Immigration, Ethnicity and Racism in Britain 1815-1945.* Manchester. Manchester University Press. ISBN: 0711900369976

Phillips, M & T. (1998) *Windrush: The Irresistible Rise of Multi-Racial Britain.* London. Harper Collins. ISBN: 00025559099

Pilkington, E. (1988) *Beyond the Mother Country. West Indians and the Notting Hill Riots.* London. Taurus. ISBN: 18504431132

Pooley and White. (1991) *Migrants, Emigrants and Immigrants.*

Ramdin, R. (1987) *The Making of the Black Working Class in Britain.* Aldershot, Gower. Wildwood House. ISBN: 0566009439

Rich, P. (1994) *Prospero's Return. Historical Essays on Race, Culture and British Society.* London. Hansib. ISBN: 1870518403

Richardson, B. (1993) *The Caribbean in the Wider World 1492-1969, A Regional Geography.* Cambridge. Cambridge University Press. ISBN: 05211359775

Roberts, A. (1994) *Eminent Churchillians.* London. Weidenfeld and Nicolson. ISBN: 0297812475

Saggar, S. (1992) *Race and Politics in Britain.* London. Harvester and Wheatsheaf. ISBN: 0745012051

Segal, R. (1995) *The Black Diaspora.* London. Faber. ISBN: 05711606611

Solomos, J. (1989) *Race and Racism in Contemporary Britain.* Basingstoke. Macmillan Education. ISBN: 033334211426

Taylor, S. (1993) *A Land of Dreams*

Tiratsoo, N. (1997) *From Blitz to Blair.* London. Weidenfeld & Nicolson. ISBN: 02977818562

Walvin, J. (1982) *Passage to Britain.*

Wambu, O. (Ed) (1998) *Empire Windrush, Fifty Years of Writing about Black Britain.* **London. Victor Gallancz.** ISBN: 0575065990

Western, J. (1992) *Passage to England, Barbadian Londoners Speak of Home.*

Williams, E. (1993) *From Columbus to Castro: The History of the Caribbean 1492-1969.* **New York. Vintage Books.** ISBN: 0394715020

Young, R. (1990) *White Mythologies. History Writing and the West.*

ARTICLES

Aspects of Britain. (1993)

Banton, M. *The Changing Position of the Negro in Britain.* **Phylon. 15.** (1953)

Davie, M. *When Peoples Move.* **Phylon. 11.** (1950).

Deakin, M. *The Politics of the Commonwealth Immigrants' Bill.* **Political Quarterly. 39.** (1968)

Duffield, I. *History and Historians in Blacks in Britain.* **History Today. September.** (1981)

Edmead, P. L. *The Decisive Decade? Caribbean Immigration into Great Britain 1948-1958, University of Birmingham M.A. Dissertation.* (1995)

Gilkes, M. *The Dark Strangers.* **In Echoes of Greatness the Making of Britain.** (1988)

Gorz, A. *The Role of Immigrant Labour.* **New Left Review. 16.** (1970)

Hunt, J. *Race Relations in Britain the Decisive Decade.* **Patterns of Prejudice. Vol 1 No 6 Nov/Dec** (1967)

Keesing's Contemporary Archives. **Vol 11** (1957-1958).

Layton-Henry, Z. *The New Commonwealth Migrants.* **History Today. December.** (1985)

Little, K. *The Position of Coloured People in Britain.* **Phylon. 15.** (1954)

Patterson, S. *Immigrants and Employment.* **Political Quarterly. 39.** (1968)

Rex, J. *Social Segregation of the Immigrants in British Cities.* **Political Quarterly. 39.** (1968)

Rich, P. *Commentary on John Bull's Island.* **History Today. September.** (1989)

Sivanandan, A. *Race, Class and the State the Black Experience in Britain.* **Race and Class. Vol. 17.** (1975-1976)

Sivanandan, A. *From Resistance to Rebellion: Asian and Afro-Caribbean Struggles in Britain.* **Race and Class. Vol. 23.** (1981-1982)

Toole, J. *GIs and the Race Bar in Wartime Warrington.* **History Today. July.** (1993)

Walvin, J. *Blacks in Britain.* **History Today. September.** (1981)

Wooldridge, A. *In Place of Fear.* **In Echoes of Greatness the Making of Britain.** (1988)

NEWSPAPERS

The Daily Mirror. Article. *'Introducing to You…The Boys From Jamaica'.* **6th September** (1958)

The Observer. Article. *'Colour'.* **23rd April** (1967)

The Times. Article. *'The West Indian Settlers'.* **9th November.** (1954)

The Times. Article. *'Foreign Workers in Britain.* **21st May.** (1951)

The Times. Series. *'The Dark Million'.* **18th to 27th January.** (1956)

The Times. Articles. **11th and 14th June** (1919)

PRIMARY ORAL HISTORIES

Mr. Linford Brock. Jamaica. (Arrival 1956)
Mr. Joe Campbell. Jamaica. (Arrival 1965)
Mr. Enos Clarke. Jamaica. (Arrival 1961)
Ms. Eloise Crichlow. Barbados. (Arrival 1958)
Mr. Frederick Dorsett. Guyana. (Arrival 1958)
Mrs. Agnes Dupont. St. Kitts. (Arrival 1957)
Mrs. Ena Edmead. St. Kitts. (Arrival 1955)
Mr. Edgar Edmead. St. Kitts. (Arrival 1955)
Mr. Charles Edmeade. St. Kitts (Arrival 1955)
Mr. Meryck Edwards. Jamaica. (Arrival 1957)
Mrs. Immelda Grant. St. Kitts - Deceased. (Arrival 1955)
Mr. Wilfred Greaves. Barbados. (Arrival 1955)
Mr. George Henry. St Kitts. (Arrival 1956)
Mrs. Lacess King. Jamaica. (Arrival 1955)
Mr. Lloyd King. Jamaica. (Arrival 1944)
Mr. Robert Mitcham. St. Kitts. (Arrival 1956)
Mr. Franklin Pencheon. St Kitts. (Arrival 1955)
Mr. Samuel 'Sonny' Philips. Nevis. (Arrival 1955)
Mr. Arnold Smithen. St. Kitts. (Arrival 1955)
Mr. Kenneth Spencer. Jamaica - Deceased. (Arrival 1954)
Mrs. Hazel Thomas. Jamaica. (Arrival 1956)
Mr. John Walters. Nevis. (Arrival 1957)
Mrs. Aldith Warner. St. Kitts. (Arrival 1955)
Mr. John 'Jack' White. Co. Tipperary. (Arrival 1934)
Mr. Ferdinand 'Motion' Williams. Jamaica. (Arrival 1954)